Made in the USA
Coppell, TX
23 July 2020

31426562R10083